EVERYDAY MYSTERIES

WHY DO ICE CUBES FLOAT?

By Benjamin Proudfit

 Gareth Stevens
PUBLISHING

Please visit our website, www.garethstevens.com. For a free color catalog of all our high-quality books, call toll free 1-800-542-2595 or fax 1-877-542-2596.

Library of Congress Cataloging-in-Publication Data

Proudfit, Benjamin, author.
 Why do ice cubes float? / Benjamin Proudfit.
    pages cm. — (Everyday mysteries)
 Includes bibliographical references and index.
 ISBN 978-1-4824-3852-9 (pbk.)
 ISBN 978-1-4824-3853-6 (6 pack)
 ISBN 978-1-4824-3854-3 (library binding)
 1. Water—Density—Juvenile literature. 2. Ice—Juvenile literature. 3. Floating bodies—Juvenile literature. I. Title. II. Series: Everyday mysteries.
 GB2403.8.P76 2016
 532.25—dc23

                                      2015033709

Published in 2016 by
Gareth Stevens Publishing
111 East 14th Street, Suite 349
New York, NY 10003

Copyright © 2016 Gareth Stevens Publishing

Designer: Katelyn E. Reynolds
Editor: Kristen Nelson

Photo credits: Cover, p. 1 successo images/Shutterstock.com; pp. 3–24 (background) Natutik/Shutterstock.com; p. 5 Digital Media Pro/Shutterstock.com; p. 7 Ewais/Shutterstock.com; p. 9 (molecule) Anzhelika Pavlova/Shutterstock.com; p. 9 (water drops) Shutterwolf/Shutterstock.com; p. 11 Kenneth Eward/BioGrafx/Science Source/Getty Images; p. 13 Serdar Tibet/Shutterstock.com; p. 15 somchaij/Shutterstock.com; p. 17 linling/Shutterstock.com; p. 19 Konstantin Shishkin/Shutterstock.com.

Printed in the United States of America

CPSIA compliance information: Batch #CW16GS: For further information contact Gareth Stevens, New York, New York at 1-800-542-2595.

CONTENTS

Boldface words appear in the glossary.

Floating Question

When it's hot outside, nothing is better than a cold glass of water. To make it stay cold longer, you can add ice! The ice floats near the top of the water. Why is that?

Density

Ice is the **solid** form of water. Water freezes, or becomes ice, at 32°F (0°C). Ice floats in water because ice is less dense than water. Density is the measurement of how much matter is in a certain **volume**.

Molecule Talk

The makeup of a water **molecule** makes ice less dense than **liquid** water. A water molecule is made from one oxygen atom and two hydrogen atoms. They're bonded, or connected, to each other.

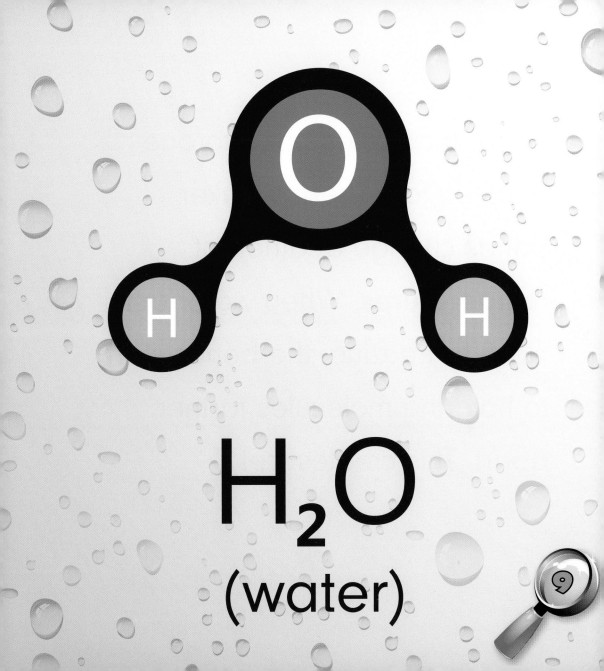

H₂O
(water)

Water molecules bond to one another, too. These weaker bonds change at different **temperatures**. When water gets close to freezing, the bonds start to hold the molecules farther apart. This creates ice!

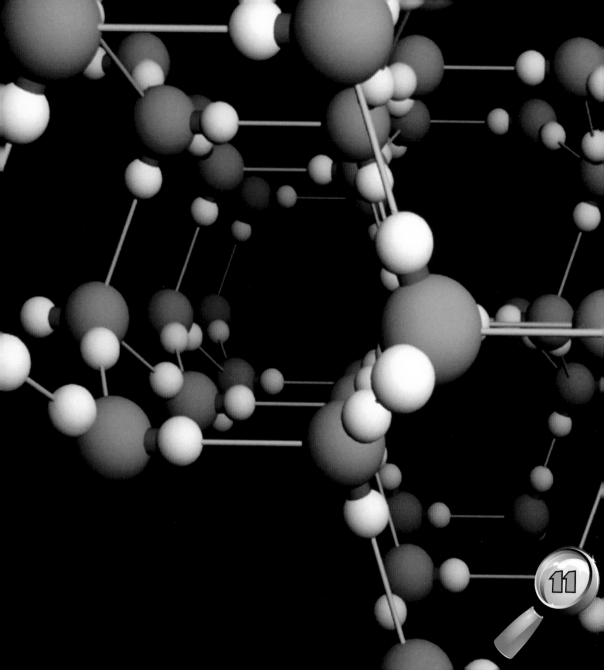

Light Ice

Have you ever seen a frozen bottle of water? You can see for yourself that the ice takes up more space than liquid water. A certain volume of ice also weighs less than the same volume of water!

When a rock is put into water, it sinks, and the water rises. The rock is denser than the water. Even though ice doesn't sink, it also **displaces** water. That's why your glass might overflow when you add ice!

Solid to Liquid

The solid form of most **substances** is denser than their liquid form. Water, though, reaches its most dense at about 40°F (4.4°C). At that temperature, water is still liquid!

16

Floating for a Reason

A frozen pond isn't frozen all the way through! Ice has formed on top of the water. This stops the rest of the water from freezing, allowing fish and plants to live under the ice!

Melt and Boil

Above 32°F (0°C), ice melts into liquid water. When warmed up, liquid water can change to a gas called water vapor. Liquid water becomes water vapor when it **evaporates**. This happens quickly when water boils!

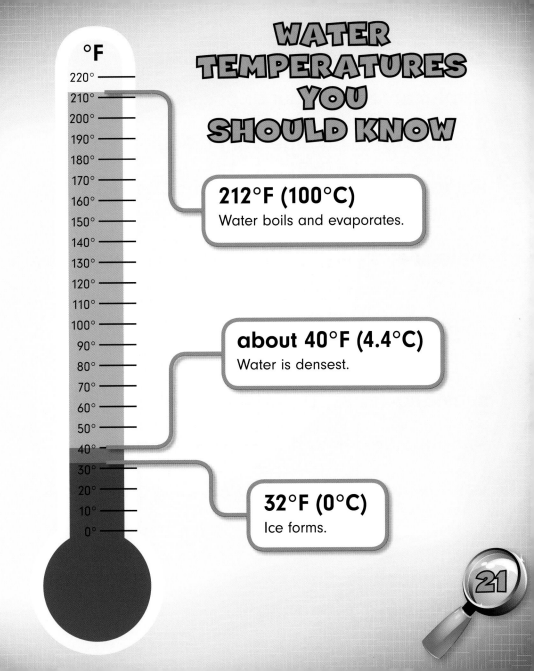

°F

220°
210°
200°
190°
180°
170°
160°
150°
140°
130°
120°
110°
100°
90°
80°
70°
60°
50°
40°
30°
20°
10°
0°

212°F (100°C)
Water boils and evaporates.

about 40°F (4.4°C)
Water is densest.

32°F (0°C)
Ice forms.

WATER TEMPERATURES YOU SHOULD KNOW

21

GLOSSARY

displace: to move out of position

evaporate: to change from a liquid to a gas

liquid: the state of matter that flows like water and isn't a solid or gas

molecule: a very small piece of matter made up of atoms

solid: the state of matter that is firm and not a liquid or gas

substance: a certain kind of matter

temperature: how hot or cold something is

volume: the amount of space an object takes up

FOR MORE INFORMATION

BOOKS

Canavan, Thomas. *Why Do Ice Cubes Float? Questions and Answers About the Science of Everyday Materials.* Mankato, MN: Black Rabbit Books, 2014.

Gardner, Robert. *Energy Experiments Using Ice Cubes, Magnets and More: One Hour or Less Science Experiments.* Berkeley Heights, NJ: Enslow Publishers, 2013.

WEBSITES

All About States of Matter
easyscienceforkids.com/all-about-states-of-matter/
Find out more about three states of matter—solid, liquid, and gas.

Changing State of Water
www.sciencekids.co.nz/gamesactivities/statematerials.html
This interactive website shows how water changes state when the temperature changes.

INDEX